Advance Reviews

"This is a gripping collection of essays and poetry that I've come back to for multiple readings. The issues are topical and riveting, and the characters are genuine and sympathetic. All of this plus clean, beautiful writing makes *Anguish in Poetry and Prose* a rare find."

> — Dr. Thomas Reilly, Professor Emeritus, Chicago State University.

"With eloquence and grace, Dr. Balter has created a fine work of art that will make you angry, perhaps make you weep, and maybe, on a few occasions, even make you smile. Whatever the emotion, readers are likely to remember his characters and contemplate the issues he raises for a long time. Beautifully written!"

> — Jeffrey Spitz, Professor, Columbia College, Chicago

"Seldom will readers find a compilation of work as well-written and engaging as Balter's *Anguish in Poetry* and Prose." Powerful and compelling, it will grab you from the first page and hold your attention throughout. Not to be missed."

> — Lawrence Block,Esq., Founder of the Highland Park Strings Orchestra and Past President of the Highland Park, IL Rotary Club

Anguish
In Poetry and Prose

Anguish
In Poetry and Prose

Alan Balter

Apprentice
House Press
Loyola University Maryland

First Edition

Paperback ISBN: 978-1-62720-296-1
Ebook ISBN: 978-1-62720-297-8

Printed in the United States of America

Acquisitions & editing by Kelly Lyons
Cover design by Chelsea McGuckin
Promotion plan by Jessica Tacconi

Published by Apprentice House Press

Apprentice House Press
Loyola University Maryland
4501 N. Charles Street
Baltimore, MD 21210
410.617.5265
www.ApprenticeHouse.com
info@ApprenticeHouse.com

Additional Works by Alan Balter

Non-Fiction

Divided Apple: A Story About Teaching in Chicago

Learning Disabilities: A Book for Parents

Fiction

Birds of a Feather

Holden and Me

Different Ways of Being

Poetry

Poems for My Grandchildren and Everyone Else's

Melancholia: A Chapbook

Dedicated to

Lisa and Tony Balter
Jessica and Max Balter

Elizabeth Mcnamara
Cole Stremmel
Nick, Luke, and Zach Mcnamara

Contents

Mother Wants to Die

Miriam wants to die. I want her to die, too. Her doctors say she's had a series of strokes. "Transitory ischemic attacks" is their medical term. They don't call people "senile" anymore; instead, they call her "demented." I call her "Mother."

She lives in a nursing home with seventy-five others. They have roommates, take their meals in a central dining hall if they are ambulatory, sit in front of a large screen television set in the day room, and participate, more or less, in various therapeutic activities. But hardly anyone talks, and nobody touches. They occupy the same time and space; yet, they're essentially alone. They're alone, and some of them, like Mother, want to die. Only thing is, we won't let them.

I visit her two or three times a week. We sit in the day room where a toothless woman sings a shrill version of "God Bless America," ending with a gummy smile and bowing to nobody in particular when she's done. A gentleman sporting an incongruous smoking jacket and an ill-matching ascot commands his dog Buddy, invisible to the rest of us, to fetch. A third repeats "Ah Ooh Ga," as if she were a horn on an antique car. Heads bob and weave to unheard rhythms, marking the beat back to childhood, I suppose.

Some moan and some giggle; in either case, without apparent reason. Others wave their arms in futile attempts to repel whatever it is that frightens them. Most sit quietly in their wheelchairs, rocking the hours away, somewhere

1

between consciousness and oblivion. And always, there is the smell—a commingling of feces, industrial strength detergent, urine, and air freshener that lingers in my nose long after I leave. I hate these visits, but if I miss one, my guilt lingers, too.

Mother once smiled when she saw me, but now she sits, eyes vacant and expressionless. She has no recollection of significant events, even the death of her beloved husband. Not long ago, after looking at each other in silence for a while, I asked her to tell me what she was thinking. She asked why "Daddy" didn't come to see her anymore and if he had found another woman. I explained, as I had many times before, that Daddy had died eighteen years ago. She had forgotten that he went to sleep one night and died with dignity and without pain. It was at the precise moment of my father's death that she began to die herself.

After her time of mourning, her memory began to slip. She forgot to pay her bills; she forgot to take her medication, and she forgot to bathe. A beautiful and meticulous woman became slovenly. Soon, she couldn't drive her car, manage her money, prepare her meals, or do her laundry. Her loss of independence terrified her. "Help me," she wailed, over and over again. Sadly, her tears did nothing to wash away the accumulation of plaque that was strangling the connections between her neurons.

Mother had another stroke that left her with slurred speech and little use of the right side of her body. She was incontinent and confined to a wheelchair. She knew she would have to leave her home, and it was the first time she said she wanted to die. When she told me she wasn't brave

2

enough to kill herself, I thought about helping her. But, I wasn't brave enough either.

On a dank day in October, we took Mother to a nursing home. We met her roommate. We talked with a social worker and occupational therapist. We hung family pictures on the walls of her room. We set a picture of Daddy on her nightstand. We wept. Indeed, for the next seven years, Miriam slowly deteriorated in front of our eyes, and we wept.

Mother's new home was clean, and the caretakers were kind. On more than a few occasions, I wondered why anyone would choose to do this kind of work, given that their charges were often removed from reality, sometimes angry and irascible, and frequently soiled themselves. Yet, they showed up for their shifts, day after day, when, in fact, they could have worked at any number of jobs for the same minimum wage.

At home one evening, I watched a television series about crime and punishment. One episode described a thirty-seven-year-old serial rapist and pedophile living on death row for more than a decade. The great state of Texas was required to provide lawyers to appeal his death sentence. To no avail, they asked jurists in the state supreme court for a reduction to life in prison without parole. Finally, the appeals process ended, and his execution was at hand. While his last meal grew cold, he told a minister he was ready. "I have no joy; I have no life; I would rather be dead," he said.

Execution is by lethal injection in Texas. The host of the series was a witness, and he described the event:

He was strapped to a gurney to immobilize his limbs.

A doctor and priest ministered to him as he was wheeled into the chamber. A needle was inserted into his arm, and he said nothing when asked if he had any last words. The intravenous was turned on and the poison flowed to his brain. After one audible gasp and a twitch, he stopped breathing. It looked as if he had drifted off, unafraid and comfortable, much like a young child taking his afternoon nap. Someone drew the blinds, and I went home.

Of course, we could have forced him to live out the rest of his wretched life, without joy, looking at pictures on the walls of his room, and growing progressively demented. Instead, we helped him die. A serial rapist and pedophile told us he would rather be dead, and we helped him die.

I wonder why we can't act with similar humanity toward our sweet mothers?

Mother Never Smiles

Bobby Lee raped five women and slashed them to the bone,
and while his last meal cooled greasy on a tin plate,
a portly priest held him close and listened:

"I have no joy, no comfort, no hope, and I'd rather be dead,
so let their poison flow that I might rest, maybe in peace,"
and we did.

Mother wants to die too, but no one listens,
so she rocks in her chair day after day
and stares through dead eyes at pictures
of loved ones, long forgotten, on the wall.

and never smiles or laughs or has any hope
and takes nourishment through a feeding tube
and has yet another stroke that renders her still
and lies in stench until someone changes her diapers
and waits for her husband, twenty years dead, to visit
and gags on mind numbing drugs forced upon her
and thinks she's in a prison
and says "help me" a thousand times over,
and we don't

why is it, I wonder, that we help murderers and rapists find peace,
but we won't do the same for our sweet mothers?

What Have We Become?

We capture and remove them from their natural habitats, put them in cages where they pace until they are insane, smash their skulls and leave them to rot on the ice, and skin them for their fur that nobody needs.

We cut off their penises and horns and sell them for aphrodisiacs, rip off their heads while they are still alive, and force them to live on manure coated concrete floors in sheds so crowded they cannot move.

We declaw them, a procedure as painful as amputating a person's fingers without anesthetic, infect them with diseases they would never normally contract, open their brains and make them suffer seizures, and force-feed chemicals to them.

We conduct repeated surgeries on them, implant wires in their brains, crush their spines, and beat them so they will learn to perform silly tricks for us.

We euthanize them by inserting electrical rods into their anuses, blind them by splashing household chemicals and cosmetic products onto their eyes, and train them to fight others of their species until they bleed and die.

These things we do to our beautiful animals.

With specific reference to baby seals, ninety-eight percent of whom are under three months of age, more than 300,000 of them are clubbed to death in an annual slaughter of marine mammals. For as far as the eye can see, dozens of tough guys with clubs, "sealers," they're called, walk the Canadian and

Norwegian ice flows in spiked boots in search of seals weighing between nine and twelve pounds who bark and have cute faces. With one or two blows to the head, sealers crush their skulls, sometimes leaving the young animals in convulsions. Estimates indicate that almost half are skinned while they are still alive. The sealers drag the bodies to fishing vessels, and the skins will ultimately be sold to skilled craftsmen who turn them into fur coats to keep fashionable ladies warm.

Sealers have a choice when it comes to how they murder. They can shoot the infants with a rifle or shotgun. This is not the preferred method, however, because bullet holes reduce the monetary value of the pelt. Also, with climate change, the ice floes are melting, so sealers often shoot from boats. The boats are in motion as are the seals, making for a tough shot; thus, many pups are wounded and left to suffer, crawling through their own blood on the ice floes.

A second method requires shattering the baby's skull with a blunt club, sort of like a baseball bat. According to statute, such clubs must be at least two feet long, I guess to generate enough bat speed to insure a sufficient degree of cranium crushing.

Finally, they can crush infant brains with a hakapik, a five-foot wooden pole with a metal spike attached to the end. Most sealers prefer the hakapik, because it's easier to aim the death blow directly at the skull; thus, one swing usually does it without too much mess.

For pups tough enough to survive the first blow, Canadian law requires that sealers continue clubbing the seal in the forehead until they're certain it's dead. They attain this level of certainty by feeling the cranium beneath the skin and blubber to determine if it has caved in to a sufficient degree, whatever the hell that is. Or, if they really want to be certain the little guys have croaked before they start skinning them, they do a "blink" test; that is, they touch the seal's eyeball. If it blinks, they've got to get back to business and finish clubbing. So far, there hasn't been a single incident during which the baby seal rose up and clubbed back.

As we have regressed toward what seems like the ultimate degree of sadism, tourist companies have begun offering "fun holiday vacations" so amateur killing enthusiasts can join in. "Yessir, step right up ladies and gentlemen because for just a few kroner, we'll fly you to Norway where we guarantee you'll be able to murder at least one totally defenseless creature and learn how to strip him clean of his fur that nobody needs. And, if you sign up within the next twenty-four hours, we'll include a free, glossy, eight by ten, color photo of you and your seal so you can show it to your friends back home.

What have we become, one must wonder?

The Hunter

the hunter slinks from the deck of his ship
to sneak up on an infant and crush his skull
he murders one whose essence colors the snow,
a mixture of bright blood and brains

who is this vicious predator
but an author of obscenity without an editor
who peels pelts from pups still breathing
then clubs the life from his brothers?

he's known as a "sealer" in the trade
a truly brave guy who stalks
dreaded, man eating, bundles of fur
who weigh twelve pounds and bark

he hauls still babies back to the ship
knowing three or four will make a fur coat
to warm a lady of substantial means
and her insubstantial soul

so here's to you, vile hunter man,
a coward with a killing tool
keep sailing your ship on the northern seas
until a cyclone blows you to hell

Jimmy, the Homeless Guy

It was a time when people talked to each other instead of texting. There were more people than guns, and AIDS and Alzheimer's were unheard of. Most moms didn't have to work. Fewer kids went to bed hungry. And, only a small number of people were homeless. Only Jimmy and a few others slept in the park.

Most of my friends steered clear of Jimmy as if he carried a dreaded disease. His clothes were filthy, and his hair fell to his shoulders in an oily mass. A Z-shaped streak scarred his temple. Two of his front teeth were missing, and the others were stippled with brown spots. If he got close, a funky smell followed him like a loyal dog. Nobody should ever smell that bad.

Along with this bundle of nasties, Jimmy spit a lot; "hockers," he called them. He put his thumb to one nostril, honked like a goose, and let fly with a clot of mucous. He wiped away any excess with his shirtsleeve. To complete the picture, he talked to himself, at times gesturing wildly and looking over his shoulder as if someone were chasing him. In sum, Jimmy did not exhibit the kind of demeanor one looks for in a potential son-in-law.

Jimmy's workplace was on the corner of Fifth and Hamlin Avenues, on the western edge of Garfield Park in Chicago. His hours were dawn to dusk, and I'd see him in the afternoon when I walked back and forth to school. In one hand, he carried a plastic cup, and in the other, a cardboard sign that read: "Please help me. I fought in the war. I have no home." One of our less sensitive citizens yelled, "Hey Dirtbag! Whose side were you on?" Jimmy showed him one of his fingers and spit at him.

At night, Jimmy retreated to his quarters underneath a viaduct. Before turning in, he stopped at the corner liquor store to buy what he needed the most. When the weather turned cold, he donned a ratty army jacket and crawled into his cardboard foxhole—a man-sized box that had previously housed a Maytag refrigerator. In the morning, he did his best to clean up in the restroom at a fast food place. If he had any leftover coins, he had some coffee.

Whenever I saw Jimmy, I smiled and said, "Hi." If I had a few extra cents in my pocket, I put them in his cup. When I gave him a pair of gloves and an old scarf wrapped around a bar of soap, he said, "Thanks kid, you're all right."

After a while, Jimmy and I began to talk. I'd be walking home from school, and he'd be sitting at the curbside taking a rest break from his daily routine. "Tell me about the war," I asked him one afternoon. "Were you in the army or what?"

"I was in Germany jumpin' outta C47s with the 101st airborne," he said. "Spent more than three years killin' Krauts. Got me a purple heart, too. See this scar? I took some shrapnel in the head. Went right through my helmet, and I been a little off ever since, if ya know what I mean."

"Did all of your buddies make it home?" I asked.

"None of 'em," he said, after taking a particularly deep swig from a bottle wrapped in a brown, paper bag. "I seen one of 'em croak right in my arms, with his brains and eyeballs spillin' all over my sleeves. And I seen another one tryin' to stuff his guts back into his stomach after he took one right there. I still dream about it, too, with the night sweats and the shakes, and the screamin' I can't get outta my head. Grown men callin' out for their moms and God is what I'm talkin' about. It's all clear as day, almost like they was still right here in front of me. Sweet Jesus; I mean right here in front of me."

Next day, I invited Jimmy to walk over to the school yard and watch one of our ball games. "Maybe you could ump," I said.

"I played some ball back in high school," Jimmy said. "I was fast and had good hands, so I played left field. Never dropped a ball neither; I mean, if I could reach it, I caught it."

"So you'll come then? We start on Sunday at about 10."

"I'd like to," Jimmy said, "but last time I was there, at the schoolyard, I mean, one of them neighbor ladies called the cops, 'cause she thought I was a pervert or somethin' lookin' to mess with the little girls and boys at school. If you're by yourself and dirty, that's what people think, I guess. I really don't need that shit. Besides, I don't get no paid vacation days, and I need to work my corner."

"Did you ever think about trying to get a real job? I asked.

"I had one last summer," Jimmy said. "It wasn't much, just pickin' up trash in the park, but I'd get the visions when I couldn't have a drink, and they canned me. I couldn't blame em; who wants to work with a guy who talks to himself and can't stay sober?"

Our family went to Michigan for the summer, and when we got home, I looked for Jimmy on his corner. I couldn't find him, so I checked under the viaduct, but he wasn't there either. When I saw another guy crawl out of the cardboard box, I got a real bad feeling.

"Excuse me Mister," I said. "Where's Jimmy?"

"He drank some antifreeze last week. It made his brain swell up, and he croaked during the night," the guy said. "My bet is that they took him to the county morgue. It's where the cops take stiffs that have no kinfolk. If nobody claims 'em after a while, they just dump 'em in a grave somewhere. That's what I heard, anyways."

We had a game the next morning. I dropped a couple of fly balls and went zero for four at the plate. A terrible day, but better than Jimmy's.

"Post-Traumatic Stress Disorder" used to be called "Shell Shock."

Anybody Home?

Jimmy and his mates stormed a beach
streaked with blood red sand
unsure whether to curse or pray,
he fell to his knees among severed limbs
and intestines, still steaming

back home, Jimmy slept in a cardboard box
that once housed a Maytag fridge
only to suffer night sweats and flashbacks
of empty eye sockets teeming with maggots

with his purple heart, paranoia, and one pair of socks
Jimmy took his breakfast under the overpass
a couple of pills, whatever the hell they were
washed down by three ounces of yesterday's wine

he toiled with a tin cup on a crowded corner
among people who looked away from his
once handsome face, and at dusk he tallied
his take home pay, ten quarters and a few dollars

he spent his earnings at the liquor store
on what he needed the most
then shared a swig with each of his mates
in a futile attempt to purge the night horrors

Jimmy died yesterday in his room for one
from an overdose of antifreeze that made his brain swell
Russell grabbed his coat, and Thomas took his socks,
and a guy named Johnny moved into the box

Rose and Me

We were playing under a wooden porch that led from our apartments to the back yard. Someone had discarded a beat up card table, and Rose had a blanket she draped over it. She invited me to play in her "fort" where we could hide from the bad guys.

"How old are you?" she asked.

"I'm four."

"Well, I'm five," she said.

"Yeah, well I'm really six."

"Me too," she countered, "but tomorrow, I'll be seven."

Our string of fibs ended when her mother, fearful we might suffocate, removed the blanket. Rose cried, so I did, too. To soothe us, her mom brought out a fresh baked cannoli. *"Mangia, miel bambini."* "Eat, my children," she said. We each got half, and we laughed hysterically when we took turns licking the other's.

Rose and her family lived in a third floor apartment facing the street. I remember her well. Her skin was golden, almost as if she had acquired a permanent sun tan. Her hair hung straight to her shoulders and was dark, too, except for a curious white streak on her forelock. Usually, she wore a colored headband to keep her bangs from falling over her forehead. She had bright blue eyes that were shielded by thick lashes. Her lips were full, and when she smiled, she showed her brilliant white teeth.

Unlike most of the girls of the era, Rose liked to play sports. She moved gracefully, had excellent eye-hand coordination, and she was strong. Had my boyfriends allowed her to join us in our softball games, I'm certain she would have held her own. Instead, her game of choice was tennis, and she took ballet lessons, too.

Most of the kids in the apartment building had birthday parties, and every year I invited Rose to mine. At my twelfth, it occurred to me that she was the most beautiful girl I had ever seen. No longer was I so interested in pulling her hair as I was in being her boyfriend. I was fortunate in having an older sister to advise me. "Why don't you take her on a date?" she asked. "You could go to lunch and a movie." My recall isn't perfect, but I think I said something like: "Hey Rosie. Wanna go to the show and get sumpin' to eat?"

I wore some of my best clothes and a pair of new shoes right out of the box. I even slicked down my hair a little and splashed on a few dabs of dad's aftershave lotion. "Oooh whee," Sis said. "Take a look at my handsome brother!"

Any degree of "cool" I had vanished when Rose greeted me at the front door of her apartment. I hadn't seen her very often in fancy clothes, and her dress was bright yellow, the same color as her headband. It's strange, but after all this time, I still remember how good she smelled.

After the movie, I took Rose for pizza. We both liked it with Italian Sausage on top, so I ordered a large one. I'd never seen anyone eat pizza with a knife and fork instead of just picking up a slice and going at it, so I figured I'd do what Rose did. She told me she thought I was a good ballplayer, and she liked to watch me play. I asked her if I could come to one of her ballet lessons. We talked some more, mostly about school, then I paid the bill and we left.

On the walk home, Rose and I held hands. On the way, we passed Jimmy, a homeless guy I knew who was working his corner asking for spare change. When he saw us, he gave me a toothless smile and a thumbs up. I'm sure he liked my taste in dates. Fess and Head, a couple of guys from the neighborhood, saw us too, and, like most kids, they were plenty quick to tease. I didn't mind, because I knew they were jealous and would have changed places with me in a flash.

We took a shortcut through the alley to the backyard. I walked her all the way to the door of her apartment and told her what a good time I had on our date. Rose put her arms around my neck and kissed me on the lips. It was my first time.

Fifteen minutes later, back in a tee shirt, shorts, and gym shoes, I was tossing a softball around with a couple of guys in the backyard. Rose came out, and I flung her one. She handled it with ease and threw it back, a perfect strike, with some heat on it.

Many people scoff at the notion of children falling in love, but Rose and I surely did. There wasn't a day we didn't see each other. We walked in the park and found places where we could neck. We did our homework together, and we played sports. She taught me how to play Jacks, and I taught her how to spin a top. I went to one of her ballet lessons, and I was amazed at how gracefully she moved. We went to Cohen's Deli on the corner and split chocolate shakes. Soon, we were best friends. Her mom and dad liked me, too.

During the summer of 1952, there was a polio epidemic. People who keep track of such things said there were over 60,000 cases. Three thousand people died, and Rose was one of them. It's when I learned about grief.

I was so sad I couldn't eat or sleep. I just paced in circles around the living room all night, and when Mom came out of the bedroom to hold me, I sobbed. "How can this be?" I asked. "She was my best friend, and I loved her so much."

Mom and Dad came with me to the funeral chapel. I knew I needed to go up to the front and tell Rose's parents that I was sorry. I waited in line until it was my turn, and when Rose's mom saw me, she held me close and whispered, "*Ora, lei ti ama in cielo.*" It means, "Now, she loves you in heaven." Then I cried, again. I couldn't help it, and I cried. So did Fess and Head and the rest of the guys who were sitting in the third row. Jeez, I never thought I'd see all those tough guys cry, especially all at once.

I mourned for a long time and even spoke to a doctor about it. We talked about the stages that people go through when they're grieving a loved one who has died. For the most part, I got over it, but a part of Rose will always be with me, as I think it should.

Later, while courting the woman who became my wife, I told her about my first love. When she heard the story, tears rolled from her bright blue eyes down over her suntanned, golden cheeks. Then she smiled, her full lips parting over her brilliant white teeth.

With All My Heart

we raked maple leaves into mounds
and rolled around in them, Rose, with
coal black hair and a silver streak
on her forelock and me, in torn jeans
and a Cubs' shirt with "Ernie" on the back

on the court and at the barre, she moved
with natural grace, elegantly as a swan,
and she was more beautiful than any girl
I had ever seen.

we went to the movies and for pizza later on,
and on the way home we held hands until we
reached her front door, and I didn't know what to do

Rose came close, put her arms around
my neck and kissed me on the lips,
my first time, and I've never forgotten
her scent and taste

after long walks in the park, we rested
under a weeping willow where we held
each other close and talked about all the
sweet things that life would bring us

now, I'm old and tired, but I still warm
when I think about Rose, forever my girlfriend,
with blue eyes and caramel colored skin,
who taught me how to love someone
with all my heart

My Friend, Michael

I met Michael during rush week, ten days into the fall term. At the time, we were both living in the same dormitory, and we were interested in pledging a fraternity. Like many other freshmen, we had heard that fraternity life provided some advantages including better food, easier contact with sorority girls, and more opportunity to participate in athletic events. As it turned out, we both pledged the same fraternity; in fact, when we moved into the house for spring term, we were roommates.

In a house with sixty guys, give or take a few, there will be all kinds. Some will be gifted academically, able to get A's with very little effort. Others will be socially adept, "face-men," they're called, who are popular with the ladies and have little trouble getting dates. Finally, there will be "Jocks," the athletically gifted who excel in sports competition and bring recognition and trophies to the house. Michael and I were all three, and we became inseparable. It was interesting because there was never competition between us; instead, each of us rooted for the other to succeed.

We never cut class, and we completed our assignments on time. Any spare time we had, we devoted to chasing coeds or exercising. The two of us took our share of space on a wide, green field between a warehouse and a stand of sugar maples either tossing spirals to each other or catching fly balls the other had hit. Afterward, we would go for beers, hoping to meet a beautiful young coed or two who had just previously admired our sweaty bodies. Damn, it was fun. In fact, it was just what college is supposed to be.

As a reward for good grades, Michael's dad gave him a used Studebaker. Thus, during our junior and senior years, we had wheels as well as having a place to swap spit with nubile sorority girls. Often, it was a foursome, and we took turns in the back seat. It was preferred, because there was no steering wheel to inhibit our moves. The campus police came to know us after a while, and it became, "You guys again; if ya park it at the football field, we'll leave ya alone." We did, and they did.

Michael and I graduated at the top or our class and were accepted at a prestigious law school. We were both awarded scholarships, and with some help from home, we were able to share a two-bedroom apartment near campus. We worked hard and partied hard, and we finished in the top five of our class. During our last year, we were co-editors of the Law Review. This, along with our grades, made it easy for us to get jobs; in fact, recruiters for some of the best law firms sought us out. We took jobs at the same firm.

We worked long hours, won some big cases, and by age thirty-five, we were promoted to full partners. This secured our financial futures, and within six months of each other, we took the plunge. Of course, each of us was best man at the other's wedding. We bought homes on the same block, and we were active in the community. Michael served as a trustee on the park district board, and I was elected to the school board.

Michael and his wife Julie had twin sons, while Amy and I had a boy and a girl born fifteen months apart. Our families were very close. We saw each other almost every day, and once a year, we vacationed together. We had other friends, nice people whose company we enjoyed, but none as close to us as Michael and his family.

There was nothing that happened that we didn't share: good times like our children's birthday parties and school related achievements; bad times like the deaths of our parents and illnesses in our children. Gradually, we became a family of eight, and a close one at that.

So it was for the next thirty years. The kids grew up, married, and we were blessed with a bunch of grandchildren. How fortunate we were because all of them were healthy without any indication of developmental problems. I liked to think that Michael and I contributed our fair share of good genes; whatever it was, the grandkids were quick learners, healthy, and a joy to be around. Life was good.

When Michael turned seventy, the trouble began. Amy and I, along with other friends, hosted a birthday celebration for him. The evening included dinner and dancing, and toward the end of the festivities, Michael rose to speak. Given so many years of practicing law, he had honed his public speaking skills to the point that many of his courtroom adversaries referred to him as a "golden tongued warrior." This night, however, he spoke slowly, slurred his words, and left long pauses between his sentences. Afterwards, I asked him if everything was all right, and he said, "I'm not sure; maybe I had one too many."

It wasn't too much booze; in fact, Michael had a stroke. His speech became almost unintelligible, and he had a weakness on the right side of his body. After seventy years of being perfect, it was difficult for him to accept that he wasn't. He sunk into a deep depression with all the classic symptoms. He didn't care to work, and he lost interest in interacting with his family and friends. He had no appetite for food or sex. He had trouble sleeping and grew slovenly because he refused to shower or shave. He couldn't make decisions, even simple ones, and he didn't care to go out. He would see me, but when I visited, he sat quietly on a chair in his family room and didn't initiate any conversation. He tried not to cry, but he did. I held him and cried too.

Things got worse very quickly. Soon, he couldn't manage his finances, drive his car, or keep himself clean. Julie called me one evening, alarmed because she couldn't find him. Our family found him an hour later wandering aimlessly through the neighborhood. A week later, I learned that he had forgotten the names of his grandchildren and no longer knew who they belonged to when looking at their photographs. He developed some strong beliefs about things that clearly weren't true. One night, for example, he pulled me aside and insisted that China had launched some nuclear missiles and that World War III had begun. When I attempted to dissuade him, he became very agitated and angry.

Of course, I wasn't a physician, let alone a neurologist, but it was clear to me that Michael was sinking into dementia. Call it what you like: "senility," "Alzheimer's Disease," or whatever, a plaque in Michael's brain was clogging the connections between his brain cells, and there was no way to flush it away.

Michael and his family leaned on us for support and assurance. We were helpless though, and as time went by, he withered before our eyes, regressing all too quickly from a self-assured, superior specimen of humanity to a person who was totally dependent upon caretakers in order to survive. Initially, Julie took care of him, then a series of twenty-four hour, seven day a week nurses, and finally, the kind staff at a residential facility for Alzheimer's cases.

Julie was a very strong person, but on occasion, she wept. "I don't think he knows me now," she said. "And I don't think he's Michael anymore. I mean, it looks like him on the outside, but inside, I think he's left us. God forgive me, but I know he wouldn't like to live the way he is."

Michael lived another four months at the nursing home. I visited him every day. The nurses thought he didn't recognize me, but I knew differently. I knew differently because when I held his skeletal hand, a crooked smile played around his lips, and he squeezed me. It was a weak squeeze, just strong enough to let me know he was there.

What a fine and graceful gentleman he was. If you have one friend like Michael in your entire life, you are very lucky. Cherish him for as long as you can. Let him know that you love him, for when he leaves, you'll miss him.

I miss my good and dear friend Michael. Every day I miss him.

You Still Know Me

once they would have called you "feeble minded"
or "senile," but now they say you're "demented"
not that it matters to me my friend,
because I call you Michael

the nurses say you don't know me
but when I hold your quaking hand in mine
and a crooked smile plays around your lips
I know they're mistaken

not long ago we played our games
between sugar maple trees and a red brick building
where they warehoused sheets of metal for some war
instead of once brilliant men

and the day after, we went to college
where we learned the law yet still found time
to write poetry for pretty coeds with blond hair
and full lips who loved us in your rusty Studebaker

then somehow, it became today
and I've come to visit you, as I will tomorrow,
and your eyes will brighten because you still know me
my good and dear friend Michael

The Joy of the Game

I'm old now—almost eighty—and like many my age, my mind wanders back to the time when I was young. Or, it just wanders.

I remember young girls with pony tails and short shorts, the unkempt man with grease stains on his shirt who walked the alley peddling rags and old iron, Cohen's Candy Store on the corner of Fifth and St. Louis, and watching Milton Berle on the neighbor's ten-inch TV screen with twenty others. It was either a Zenith or a Muntz.

I remember a gray, 1940 Dodge with running boards, food rationing to support the war effort, my mother's spaghetti sauce, my body—lean as a blade and firm—and my friends, loyal and true, many of whom are gone now. Like so many of my vintage, however, I seldom remember what I had for breakfast. It doesn't matter much.

My boyfriends and I played together in the yard at the rear of our apartment building. There was no grass, just a dirt surface surrounded by a blue, wooden fence. When rain muddied the yard, we moved our games to the adjacent alley, or to the schoolyard, about a mile from home. At school, the playground was covered with gravel, an abrasive that was good for scraping skin from knees and elbows. A chain link fence separated the school yard from the rest of the neighborhood. We could have easily walked through the gate, but we chose to climb it and tear our jeans instead.

We played every sport, but slow pitch, sixteen-inch softball was our obsession. We played it every day except when it snowed or was too cold. Our games were not scheduled; we just showed up after school or on weekends and chose sides. We cut cardboard squares for bases, and we chipped in for the ball, a "Clincher," that set us back fifteen cents each. It lasted about a month before splitting and spilling its innards.

Out of the box, the Clincher was a thing of beauty—pure white, tightly seamed, and, during the first couple of innings before it was knocked around some, as hard as granite. Mitts were for "sissies" and banned from use. Similar disdain was directed toward anyone who backed away from a line drive. We went for it no matter what; in fact, bandages over bruised and swollen fingers were badges of distinction. Some of us wore them to school as a matter of course, even when our fingers hadn't been injured.

Teams had ten players, the usual nine, plus a short center fielder who positioned himself behind second base, close enough to field grounders hit up the middle and far enough to snag bloopers hit to the outfield. When only nine guys showed up, a team did without a short center fielder, or sometimes, the opposing team supplied a catcher.

Teams were chosen by captains, typically the two best players in the neighborhood. Everyone knew who they were. A coin toss determined who got first pick; then, they took turns making their choices until everyone was chosen. It was a swift and merciless process that showed us precisely where we ranked in the eyes of our peers. No one cared about the self-esteem of those picked toward the end except for those who were picked toward the end.

Uniforms varied. While still in grade school, we changed our school shoes for sneakers and wore what we had worn to school. On a warm weekend day, it was shorts and a tee shirt, although those who were into puberty sometimes went shirtless to advertise their burgeoning biceps and pectorals. By ninth grade, most wore athletic pants of various colors with a stripe down the outer seam. We bought our first pair of spiked shoes and practiced knocking mud from our cleats with a bat, even when there wasn't any. A few wrapped colorful bandanas around their foreheads, supposedly to absorb excess perspiration, but it was mostly for the look.

Some of our guys enjoyed heroic reputations. Fat Sam, for example, weighed about 250 but stood only five feet, six inches tall. His stature, plus a low slung butt, resulted in a center of gravity similar to a sequoia. When he connected, the ball soared out to left or center field. The outfielder, already hard against the chain link fence, watched as it flew over his head, and most of the time, the ball was still going up.

Sam hit some truly prodigious shots, one hitting the "M" on the sign of Mel's Tobacco and Liquor store across the boulevard from the playing field. Mel, who was sweeping the sidewalk in front of his business establishment, saw the ball ricochet off his sign and bounce off his cat, heretofore dozing in the sun. Mel cheered, and the cat hissed.

Fat Sam preferred to play third base, but when he was tired, he took his position behind the plate, where a minimum of running was required. While guarding home plate one afternoon, an opposing player tagged up at third base with the idea of scoring after a fly ball to left field. The left fielder threw a strike to home, and Sam was waiting with the ball cupped firmly in both hands and cradled tightly against his abdomen.

The baserunner barreled into Sam, assuming that such a tactic might dislodge the Clincher from Sam's grasp. The collision resulted in his staggering halfway back to third base where he fell and lay twitching on the ground, as if possessed. All the while, he alternated between calling for his mother and God until he regained consciousness. Sam picked him up, shook his finger to admonish him never to try that again, and handed him his hat.

Sam's reputation was well-deserved, although it's probable that his legend was somewhat tainted by hyperbole as time passed. One of our guys, "Head," we called him for the unusually large size of his cranium, swears he remembers Sam smashing a new Clincher into a drainage ditch, a good 300 feet from home plate. Howie recalled an incident where a shot off Sam's bat took the head "clean off" a pigeon who had, to Birdy's eternal misfortune, wandered near third base. Somehow the ditch got further and the pigeon morphed into a hawk as time passed.

Fat Sam went on to graduate with honors from law school. He married, had three children, and built a successful practice in real estate law. He died from kidney failure in his early fifties. A couple of us offered to donate our kidneys, but none of us had one that matched. It was the only time I saw Sam cry.

Fess was our shortstop. He was good looking and well-built with a shock of blond hair he wore to his shoulders, a style which wouldn't come into vogue until a few decades later. He was also dyslexic, a disability that complicated his progress through school. In those days, people thought kids who couldn't read were just lazy or stupid, and little help was available for them.

Truth is, Fess was anything but stupid. In fact, in some areas he was quite gifted, for example, at enlisting a string of hopeful cheerleaders to read his assignments to him and help him write his essays. Thus, he made it through high school, although it took him five years.

Fess was gifted at shortstop, too—some would say a genius. We had a one run lead in the last inning of a game against an unbeaten team from a neighboring school. They knew of us, and we knew of them, so a challenge was inevitable. The top of their lineup were due at bat, and they looked very confident, indeed smug, as they took their practice swings. I was playing left field, so I had a perfect view of all that happened in front of me.

Their first batter hit a line shot headed in my direction. I would retrieve it after a bounce or two and get the ball to second, thus holding the batter to a single. To my amazement, though, and everyone else's, Fess dashed to his right, leapt about three feet and somehow managed to snare it with one hand. Most of our opponents' smugness evaporated at the same time as their jaws dropped. And, no one could anticipate that the best was yet to come.

Their second batter hit a one hopper into the hole between short and third. Fess took a couple of steps to his right and threw the batter out with his right hand. The third guy managed a grounder that was headed up the middle until Fess drifted to his left, snatched the ball on the short hop, and threw the batter out with his left hand. He managed this feat

32

so smoothly that hardly anyone noticed that our shortstop could throw equally well with either hand. I haven't seen anyone do it since.

On the walk home after the game, I asked Fess how he did it. Like an eight-year-old musical prodigy who composes symphonies, he didn't know. His talent was just there, ready to be applied when needed.

Fess and I were roommates for a while at college where it wasn't long before he discovered he couldn't major in "Shortstop." Lengthy reading and writing assignments overwhelmed him, and he dropped out. We stayed in touch until he moved out of state, and after a few years, I stopped hearing from him. On occasion, during a losing battle with insomnia, I'll close my eyes and imagine him throwing out one batter with his right hand and the next with his left. It was artistry, no less than balletic.

I played softball until I lost a step or two and could no longer reach fly balls I once would be waiting for. For a time, I managed to prolong the inevitable by moving to first base where my deficiencies were less obvious. Finally, just past my forty-second birthday, I put the spikes in the basement and the Clincher in the closet. For the last couple of years, some of my teammates were men well into their fifties. We showed up every Sunday morning, bellies lopping over our belts, braces supporting various joints, and inevitably pulled our hamstrings while playing a semblance of the game we loved. We suffered through Wednesday, but it didn't matter much.

Today, the kids don't play sixteen-inch softball anymore. Ask any twelve-year-old what a Clincher is, and his response is likely to be a blank stare. Now, it's Little League and Pony

League, neatly organized and scheduled, on manicured fields with regulation bases, umpires, uniforms, scoreboards, and pushy parents berating coaches. Seems to me the only thing they're missing is the joy of the game.

Many of the apartment buildings on the street where I grew up have been demolished, but mine remains. The dirt yard at the rear has been covered with concrete, and a couple of abandoned and rusty Buicks stand nose to nose at one end, providing shelter for a family of feral cats. I drove by not long ago and was amazed at how small the yard appeared. Exiting my car, I stood where I used to as a boy, assumed my stance, and remembered the first time I lined a Clincher from one end of the yard to the other. It was an important rite of passage.

My Clincher remains, too, in a special place on the top shelf of my closet. Once in a while, I take it down to fondle and toss from hand to hand. It's well-scuffed but would likely survive a few more games. My name is written on it. So is Fat Sam's, Fess's, Head's, Howie's, Chubby's, Little Louie's', and the rest of them.

I don't see the guys anymore, but it would be great to share one more Sunday in the schoolyard with the sun in our faces. Give me just one more game with our cardboard bases, a new Clincher, and a body that is lean and firm again.

Snowflakes

Snowflakes swirling through the trees
Cool my lips and tongue
Transient as my memories
Of times when I was young

Once I dashed around the bases
Fleet afoot and agile
Now confined to lesser places
I'm ancient, stiff, and fragile

I dream of playing but one more time
Fat Sam and Howie and me
Just one more game in our prime
How joyous it would be

In my dreams there is no sorrow
Legs loosen and grow stronger
Dawn begins a sweet tomorrow
And snowflakes last much longer

Billy Burnside

There was a homosexual kid in the neighborhood, at least that was the prevailing opinion. With neither the knowledge nor sensitivity that comes with any degree of maturity, we labeled him. We called him names. We did this based upon a cluster of stereotypical behaviors rather than any direct evidence of his sexual preference. It may be that teenagers don't require direct evidence before they categorize people. Or, it may be that nobody does.

Of course, we didn't call Billy Burnside "gay" because, at the time, that word still meant "happy" or "cheerful." Instead, he was a "sissy boy," a "homo," a "queer," a "fairy," or a "fruit." We used those terms flippantly, with no concern for any effect they might have had on how he felt about himself. Kids can be cruel. Stupid and selfish, too.

Billy Burnside's appearance was cherubic with rosy cheeks and a short, chubby stature. His hips were broader than his shoulders, so his body looked like a pear. His hair hung over his forehead in bangs as if someone had placed a bowl over his head and cut around it. When he spoke, his voice was high pitched, and he lisped. During all the years I knew him, I never saw him in a pair of jeans; instead, he wore knickers with long stockings drawn to his knees or corduroys with suspenders. I never saw him smile much, either.

Often, he wore a white shirt with a clip-on bow tie, and he always had a pen holder with ballpoints in his shirt pocket.

Whenever we didn't have a pen of our own, we asked Billy for one of his. If he refused, we simply grabbed one. He carried a leather briefcase, too, a sure-fire way to invite scorn from his classmates. Really, who carries a briefcase in grade school except fairies and queers? Today, the terms of preference would probably be "nerd" or "dweeb." Not exactly heroic, but certainly better than anything we called Billy.

Billy usually made the honor role, and he had some talent in writing that showed up in his essays, poetry, and short stories. When he came in first in the annual school poetry contest, his work and his picture appeared in the local newspaper. His award included a series of writing lessons at a summer arts camp and a United States Government Savings Bond.

In high school, some of Billy's poems were published in the "Young Authors" literary magazine. At the awards assembly, only the teachers and a few girls applauded. I didn't win anything. Neither did any of my athletically gifted friends.

In other areas of endeavor, particularly activities that required coordination and strength of large muscles, Billy had some problems. He tripped and fell in the 100-yard dash and came in dead last. He threw a ball like a girl, not even sure of which arm to use. He couldn't manage even a single push-up or chin-up, and when required to climb a pole to the ceiling of the gymnasium, he elevated himself about a foot before collapsing in a heap at the bottom. Most everyone laughed at him.

Perhaps if there were a father at Billy's home, he might have practiced some of those things and improved. Billy lived with his mom and three older sisters, though, and I'd guess that none of them was particularly interested in tossing around a softball or climbing poles. His sisters did try to protect him from tough guys in the neighborhood, but such intervention only made things worse.

Given the constant jeers, laughter, and teasing from his classmates, both in the gymnasium and out, it wasn't long before Billy resigned and withdrew. He sat in the school cafeteria, eating lunch at a table for one. Think of it. In the noisy expanse of the school cafeteria, where kids amass in raucous groups of eight and ten in order to share their experiences and get to know each other, Billy sat mute and alone. Year after year, he sat mute and alone.

Truth is, there were times I wanted to go over and sit next to him, but I was afraid of what my friends would think. Thus, I was clearly a coward, more concerned with being accepted by my peers than in helping a kid who could have used a boost.

It would have been bad enough had our treatment of Billy been limited to isolation and teasing. But, callous and unfeeling as we were, we went even further. Tying him to a tree seemed like a humorous prank, so we did it and left him there.

It's true that my participation in Billy's debasement was limited to standing around and smirking without doing any of the actual tying. However, I did nothing to stop those who did from accomplishing their feat. Like the getaway driver in a bank heist, I aided and abetted.

Over the years, I have not forgotten what we did to Billy Burnside. In fact, the recollection remains a source of great shame. I've wondered, too, about our motivation. Perhaps, as young teenagers, still unsure and vulnerable ourselves, we needed Billy to help us solidify our own shaky positions during adolescence, a time when peer acceptance is so crucial. Whatever our motivation, what we did was flat out rotten. In my fantasy, I stand up to my peers and tell them to back off and leave Billy alone. Jeez, I only wish I had done that.

Billy Burnside shot himself in the head one afternoon after school.

Queer Billy Burnside

Billy Burnside lived with his three older sisters
a kind and gentle boy who never stepped on ants
he went to school each day and made the honor roll
among classmates who were cruel as winter

Billy didn't play sports; he found them much too rough
instead he fashioned clay sculptures of super heroes
and wrote sonnets for friends who lived in his head
but would never know him

the other guys didn't like his style so after school one day
they tied him with rough ropes to a black oak tree
where hairy caterpillars and fat, brown worms
crawled over his shoes

they left him alone and went off to play their games
until just before the sun went down when they returned
to call him a sissy boy and a fruit and taunt him
for wetting his corduroy knickers

a policeman came to free him and walk him home
this kind and gentle boy who didn't have much to say
he stumbled up the stairs and sat atop his bed
where queer Billy Burnside put a bullet through his head

Depression

My first symptom was drop foot in my left leg. My ankle was floppy, so my gait looked as if I were high stepping over low hurdles as I walked. Then, my right hand and fingers weakened. I wasn't in pain, but I was anxious because whenever things aren't perfect with me, I assume the worst. It's the "every headache is a brain tumor" syndrome.

The weakness in my fingers worsened, and at one point, I couldn't even flip a light switch. Then, I began having trouble chewing and swallowing. My anxiety level took a giant leap upward, because I knew just enough about neuromuscular diseases to recognize that my symptoms were associated with ALS (Amyotrophic Lateral Sclerosis) or Lou Gehrig's Disease. Depression bared its ugly fangs; it was there, hanging around, just waiting to lay more misery on me.

I made an appointment with a neurologist. A couple of days before my visit, I noticed that my speech was slurring, a symptom which pushed my anxiety level even higher. Also, I had bouts of double vision, and one of my eyelids drooped. I imagined becoming totally dependent upon others while I wasted away and ultimately suffocated to death. My depression deepened. Think black hole.

The neurologist did her exam and directed my wife and me to her office where we would discuss the results. "How did I do?" I asked.

"Well, we've got to do more testing," she said

"What is it, exactly, that you're testing for?"

"I've got to be concerned about ALS," she said.

A wave of cold slid down my body. In fact, I was horrified. "How can this be happening to me?"

Not long ago, I was a healthy, robust guy who had run a marathon. Now, I was going to die a horrible death, but only after I gradually morphed into a helpless glob of protoplasm. Equally dreary was the thought that my dear wife would have to watch my deterioration and wouldn't be able to do anything about it.

Things got worse. The neurologist told me that I'd have to wait a week before being tested. Of course, I would have preferred being tested immediately, but there was no chance. "The doctor who will test you is at a conference in Toronto, and she won't be back for a week," lady neurologist said. How was it, I wondered, that at a teaching hospital in a large, Midwestern city, there was only one doctor who could administer a test for ALS? "This was a unique form of torture," I thought. "They tell you you're going to die; then they send you home for a week to mull it over."

Back at home, the full force of depression hit me. I lost all interest in my hobbies; I had no appetite for food or sex, and I was tearful. I had trouble sleeping, and I had a gnawing feeling in the pit of my stomach that wouldn't go away. I grew slovenly and didn't care to shave or shower. Making decisions, even simple ones, was impossible, and I had no interest in leaving the house or seeing friends.

For the week, I lost eight pounds and took a lot of Xanax. The few hours that I slept each night were my escape, and I got angry when I awoke to face my sickening reality. If my wife would have allowed it, I'd have pulled the covers over my head and wept. I did anyway.

During the week, my wife insisted that we attend a baseball game. My grandson was playing, and should his team win, the boys would be league champions. Max hit a three-run double in the last inning to win the game. It was something he'll probably remember for the rest of his life, but I didn't see it. That's what depression does. The feelings of dread, anxiety, and sadness seal you off; indeed, I was so enveloped by my own misery that not much else got through.

At last, the week passed, and we reported to the hospital. The test took about an hour, during which time I got stuck with needles all over my body. The idea was to determine how well my nerves were carrying messages to my muscles. The doctor stuck me one last time and said, "Good."

"Does that mean I don't have ALS?" I asked.

"That's what it means," she said.

"Then what do I have?" I asked, hardly able to contain myself.

"More testing," she said.

I met my wife in the foyer, and both us just sat for a time and gave thanks.

Ultimately, I was diagnosed with myasthenia gravis. It's another neuromuscular disease; this one, however, is treatable. Indeed, the treatment was truly amazing. I took my first pill, Mestinon it's called, at 6 in the evening, and at 7 p.m., I felt darn near perfect. My strength came back, and my speech wasn't slurred. To me, it was nothing short of a miracle. I have taken those pills for almost ten years, and I have not had any relapses. If a person needs to have a neurological disease, myasthenia gravis is the one to have.

As for my depression, it gradually lifted; however, a large percentage of the general public still don't get it. They think that physical illnesses like heart disease and diabetes are real but mental illnesses aren't. Diabetics wear bracelets to make others aware of their condition, but you'll never find anyone with a bracelet that says "clinically depressed." No one is ashamed when diagnosed with cancer, but people still are when told they're bipolar. It's true, too, that there are still some health insurance companies that do not cover mental illnesses to the same extent that they cover physical illnesses.

I suspect that such primitive attitudes toward depression would vanish very quickly as soon as the ignorant ones get depressed. They will see for themselves how real it is and how debilitating it can be. My guess would be, in fact, that while wallowing in a depression, many would be very quick to trade it for any number of physical diseases. "Hey, man, I'll give you my depression for a hernia and a year's worth of migraine headaches."

It's a terrible disease, and I hope I never go there again.

Which One is Second Best?

a dismal dawn, dreary and wet
ushers in yet another day of
hollow, hopeless hours
on the lip of oblivion

a murky space is where I live
where the air reeks of rot
and dry heaves spew bloody clots
that taste sour as bile

fitful sleep is my escape
from the pounding of my pulse
still, I dream of a green eyed boy
who once played in the sun

comes sup with me, a buffet for two
at once simple and severe
an appetizer of mind altering drugs
and a main course of despair

curled into a fetal position
with my knees drawn to my chest
am I living or am I dead
and which one is second best?

Morrie and Edith

269462. It was a tattoo, faded but still legible, on Morrie's forearm. His wife Edith had one too. Both were holocaust survivors.

After the war, they settled in Chicago, and, with the help of some relatives, opened a store at the corner of Fifth and St. Louis Avenues on the west side of the city. Cohen's Candy Store and Deli became the neighborhood place where kids stopped in for "dessert" on their way back to school.

Mr. Cohen was a short man, perhaps five feet, four inches, slim, with blue eyes and a few wisps of thin, gray hair. His pallid face was wrinkled, and he wore wire-framed spectacles. He smiled a lot, particularly when kids came into the store. "Sonny" he called me. I never knew why until years later.

I'm sure he liked me, probably because he knew I was a low risk for shoplifting and was good for at least four chocolate milkshakes a week. He made them thick with chunks of ice cream still floating around. I didn't have diabetes yet.

Mrs. Cohen was nice, too. She wore her hair pulled back into a bun, and she always smelled good. Like Morrie, she wore wire framed glasses and squinted if she suspected any young hooligans were thinking about lifting some goodies from a shelf. She was taller—by at least five inches—than her husband, and she outweighed him by a good forty pounds. I never heard it happen, but I suspected that any orders she directed toward Morrie were followed by a quick, "Yes Dear."

I must have been seven or eight years old the first time I walked into the store. It was at street level in a building that had a couple of apartments above it. On the left, as one entered, there were display cases filled with penny candy. All the sugary delights were represented: root beer barrels, lemon heads, candy cigarettes, jaw breakers, Bit O' Honey, little chocolate buttons you ate off a strip of paper, and red wax lips you could chew after tiring of wearing them. A few pennies worth of such glucose laden treats every day made a lot of dentists happy. And, if I didn't have any pennies, Mr. Cohen slipped me a few goodies anyway.

The deli section was on the right. The counter was made of some kind of fake marble, and there were seven or eight chairs with well-worn seats and wooden backs. A row of salamis hung from the wall. They were anywhere from twelve to thirty-six inches in length and ranged in texture from soft through medium and hard. We always had one at home. The last inch, hard and greasy, was the most prized piece.

A half dozen tables were at the rear of the store. Groups of two or more would be seated there, and Edith provided the wait service. "So, what's it gonna be, sweetheart?" was her usual greeting supplemented by an occasional, "Talk to me, Dahlink."

A corned beef sandwich just fat enough and served thick and warm on fresh rye bread, with or without seeds, was sixty cents, and a chocolate phosphate was a dime. A milkshake, in chocolate, vanilla, or strawberry, whipped up in one of those tall, silver containers, was twenty cents, and it came with a couple of cookies on the side. At the time, no one knew about cholesterol or even remotely considered including bean sprouts, kale, or other health foods in their diets. "You wanna live and be healthy for a long time Dahlink? Have a nice corned beef sandwich every day for ninety years," Mrs. Cohen advised, a smile playing around her lips.

A heavy rain was pouring down, so I lingered in the store, savoring a chocolate milkshake while waiting for it to stop. Mr. Cohen was cleaning the counter. "Would you like a couple more cookies, Sonny?

"Sure," I said. "That would be great."

Morrie brought them to me, and as he extended his arm to set down the plate, I saw his tattoo.

"What's that?" I asked.

"That's Auschwitz," Morrie said.

I had heard of the German concentration camps, in school and at home, but Morrie was the first survivor I'd met. He spoke for more than an hour, and I listened without saying a word.

"You must never forget what I'm about to tell you," he began. "Never forget. The Nazis, may they burn in hell forever, came in the night and rounded us up like cattle. They crammed us into boxcars so crowded that no one could lie down or even sit. We rode for hours. Some people vomited, some shit, and some died. Edith and I clung to each other, frightened and praying. We were lucky to be near openings in the side of the boxcar, so at least we had some fresh air. Finally, we stopped, for we had reached Auschwitz.

"Arriving at Auschwitz was like walking into hell. The doors of the boxcars opened, and we were pulled out, in the midst of shepherd dogs showing their teeth and growling. The Nazis had rifles and whips, and their screaming distracted us for a time from the smell of burning flesh and the fires all around us. Women were wrestled away from their husbands, and I didn't know when I would see Edith again, if ever. I couldn't stop sobbing, so great was my grief. Then, we were forced to run to a building where they stripped us and put us under cold showers. No shampoo or towels were provided.

"Next, they hustled us to another building where they shaved off our hair. Prisoners who had been there for a while sprayed our bodies with disinfectant. It was yellow and burned my skin. They gave us some rags to wear and wooden clogs. During the final stop, we were taken to tables where women stood with unusual looking pens in their hands. These were the needles used for tattooing, and it is when I stopped being Morrie and became number 269462.

"Finally, we were shoved into barracks. 'At last, I can lie down,' I thought. But I couldn't. There were a thousand others, just like me, trying to get some sleep on the bunks. I was lucky to find a corner to cling to. Thus, I was in Auschwitz, an all-inclusive resort in the wilderness. No reservations were required.

"Eventually, I muscled my way to a cot that I shared with two others, not counting the rats. If we ate at all, it was some kind of gruel for breakfast and thin soup with a piece or two of mystery meat, maybe rat, floating around for dinner. Almost everyone was malnourished or sick, but those who died, in many ways the lucky ones, were quickly replaced as more boxcars rolled in.

"I lasted more than two years, with little change in routine. Of course, it wasn't long before we came to learn the horrible truth. The large rooms they told us were group showers were gas chambers where the Nazi bastards murdered hundreds of thousands of us, including little children. Then, they dumped us in mass graves. The only reason I escaped such a fate was I could keep books, and they figured I'd be useful.

"In January 1945, the Allies were coming, so the Nazis began moving us to different camps. The evacuation of Auschwitz was a death march because about 15,000 prisoners died on the way. I ate nothing but snow and became a living skeleton at about eighty pounds. When we got to areas that were too warm for snow, I survived by eating grass. So even today, I won't eat lettuce.

"I woke up one morning, and the Nazis were gone. They must have left quickly because spare uniforms hung in closets and records were still in file drawers. Cowards seldom hang around when someone stands up to them.

"When the Americans arrived in camp a few hours later and liberated us, I fell to the ground with relief. It was over-whelming, because I was finally free. Now, I could breathe fresh air without the smell of burnt flesh. I could sit outside on a chair and let the sun warm my face. I could eat tasty food in large portions.

"Of course, my beloved Edith was always on my mind. She was the last thing I thought about at night and the first thing I thought about in the morning. I held out hope that she was alive, but deep inside of me, strong as she might have been, I feared the worst.

"Three of us were sitting in the dining room enjoying a delicious pot roast, mounds of mashed potatoes with butter, and unlimited milkshakes. Our lively conversation suddenly stopped when three women walked into the room. Two of them were my buddies' wives, and the third was Edith. Chances are, Sonny, you'll never see a celebration like that one."

Edith was spared only because of her size. She was big and strong, so they put her to work planting and harvesting potatoes. During our entire time at Auschwitz, she was never more than half a mile from me. Of course, she had some rehabilitating of her own to do, but in a couple months, we were well enough to travel, and we got a free plane ride to London. A cousin gave me a job in his grocery store, and I put enough money away to fly to America—Chicago, that is— where Edith had some relatives. They lent me enough money to open this store, for which I will be forever grateful."

Mr. Cohen rubbed a hand through my hair and said, once again, "Never forget what I have told you. If anyone calls you a 'kike' or a 'Dirty Jew,' kick 'em hard Sonny, right where it hurts the most."

Eventually, Mr. Cohen announced they were closing the store. I was never sure why, but the rumor was that he and Edith were tired of the cold winters and wanted to move to a warmer climate. So, that was it, the end of an era.

Two weeks later, Mr. and Mrs. Cohen were gone. The store remained empty for a while, not a salami in sight. In the six years that followed, what had been Cohen's Candy Store and Deli became a dry cleaners, pizza parlor, record shop, and a pet store. None of them stayed in business very long. Neither did the Cohen's, I feared.

My plan was to take a streetcar east to the loop, transfer to the elevated train, and ride north to Wrigley Field, home of the Cubbies. They were mired in last place, nothing unusual at the time, but it was still a lot of fun to go to the park, have some hot dogs and peanuts, and watch them lose.

As I was waiting for the streetcar on the corner, a Yellow Cab pulled up and a man got out. I didn't pay any attention until he turned around, and I recognized Morrie. "My God," I yelled. "It's you. What are you doing here, and where is Edith?"

He hugged me and said, "How you've grown Sonny my boy; we moved to North Miami Beach when I closed the store. I had enough saved up to rent a nice apartment in a six flat building a couple of blocks from the ocean. After a year or so, the owner said we could live rent free if I would manage the building. I did small repairs, took out the trash, and collected the rent. It was a good deal that saved us hundreds a month. I bought some stock, too, and made about fifteen-thousand bucks."

"Hey, that's all great, but what are you doing here, and where is Edith?" I persisted.

"Two years ago, Edith was diagnosed with breast cancer. We tried everything like chemotherapy and X-rays, but the cancer spread to her lungs and brain. She died quietly while I held her in my arms. The last words she said were: "Be brave my dear husband; mourn for a while if you must; then go someplace where you will be happy."

"I'm so sorry," I said. "She was a nice lady, and I know how much you loved her."

"It's true," Morrie said, "I loved her like my life, and now I am back at a place where I will be happy. I'm renting the store and reopening Cohen's Candy Store and Deli. I'm going to see to it that it's exactly like it used to be, and there will always be a job in the store waiting for you."

Business thrived, and I worked there every summer I was in college. Morrie became part of our family; when he died, we helped with the funeral arrangements, including taking him back to Florida where he could rest in eternal peace next to his beloved Edith. It was my honor to eulogize him.

Edith's cousin eulogized Morrie, as well. "I will not speak of Morrie without including Edith," she said, "for over the years they merged into one. Edith and Morrie had so many good traits that it's hard to talk about only one. Surely their bravery stands out. Surviving Auschwitz is an example. Traveling to Chicago and running a business is another. And, even earlier in their lives, they were so courageous when they overcame the death of their infant child Sonny. May our dear Morrie rest in eternal peace next to Edith, a woman of valor.

For me, I shall always cherish their memories—these sweet, brave people, who made my life so much better.

Great Grandpa's Shoes

they came in darkness and ripped us from our beds to cattle
cars so crammed we couldn't sit, and our people prayed and
vomited and shit before the lucky ones died where they
stood

at last, the doors creaked open to savage men and menacing
shepherd dogs with yellow fangs dripping froth and snap-
ping and snarling as if rabies had infested their dim, canine
brains

the smell of burnt flesh befouled the air while they stripped
us naked and shaved our heads and tattooed our forearms
with black numbers to remind us they had stolen our names

they tore our wives away to rape and ravage, and our chil-
dren too, quivering in terror, and gave us black and white
striped clothes of coarse cloth at once impotent against the
bitter cold

a corps of maniacs mined our teeth for gold then castrated
and sterilized us and submerged us in icy waters, in their
insane quest for a superior race of teutonic monsters

in barracks with buckets for toilets and no water to wash,

three skeletal men shared
a straw filled mattress, and together we starved and stunk,
and stiffened before the dawn

the shoes of the old and infirm were strewn in piles before
they herded us to shower under spigots spewing poison gas,
leaving us to claw at the metal doors until our fingers bled,
and we were incinerated and stacked in mass graves, up to
six thousand souls a day

a million people with somber faces and hushed voices walk
the dimly lit halls of the museum each year to see the shoes
on display, and some of them will never forget because a pair
belonged to Great Grandpa.

Sonny Johnson

Sonny Johnson never had a chance.

His mother was an eighteen-year-old prostitute with scoliosis and a club foot. His father was a neighborhood pimp with holes in his arms from a hundred dollar a day habit. Sonny never knew them.

Four days after contributing to Sonny's conception, Father died from a combined overdose of heroin and peppermint schnapps. Seven months later, Mother squatted in the restroom at a fast food restaurant, grunted a few times, and gave birth. During her pregnancy, she never saw a doctor.

Mom was back on the street by the time a maintenance woman entered the stall and found a dirty woolen coat wrapped around a three-and-a-half-pound newborn and his bloody umbilicus. His eyes were puffy, and his head was misshapen. Much of his body was covered with fine hair, and his skin, particularly on his hands and feet, was peeling. His tiny lips and fingertips were blue from oxygen deprivation, and he was mewing like a hungry kitten.

A Johnson and Company ambulance rushed him to the nearest hospital, and it was a bright, sunny day, so the nurses named him Sonny Johnson. Doctors hooked him to a respirator, feeding tube, and heart monitor. His sucking reflex kicked in; his lungs matured, and he gained weight.

A few months passed, and when it was clear he was going to survive, Sonny was transferred to the Sisters of Mercy Children's

Home, an orphanage that struggled to stay open each year due to insufficient state and local funding. So, beyond meeting basic needs, they were unable to provide much that was enriching for their residents. Nonetheless, Sonny's life at the orphanage, while far from ideal, was better than it would have been had "Old Mother Hooker" decided to take him home.

Caretakers fed, bathed, and changed baby Sonny. They gave him all he needed to grow and survive, and never once did they mishandle or abuse him in any way. But, with so many others to care for, time for bestowing much real love and stimulation was limited. Most concerning, Sonny didn't hear a lot of organized language as he grew up. He seldom heard a bedtime story, and, as he grew, hardly anyone engaged him in one-on-one conversation. Later, his limited language skills made it difficult for him at school.

Sonny was essentially isolated as he got older. Children his age from the surrounding community never asked him to visit at their homes or join them in any sort of activity. In fact, he and his mates at the orphanage were outcasts, a surplus population never invited in as if they were carriers of smallpox or the plague.

So sheltered was he that Sonny didn't chew a piece of bubble gum until he was twelve years old. He never rode a bicycle, played monopoly, skipped rope, played ball, or spun a bottle. He learned about birthday parties, sleepovers, hanging out at shopping malls, talking on the phone, going out on dates, kissing girls, eating at restaurants, or having any sort of privacy by watching television shows or movies. Today, psychologists and social workers would likely call him "culturally deprived," "developmentally delayed," or some other term they discuss at their professional conferences.

He did attend the orphanage school, as required, until he was graduated at age eighteen, but in basic academic subjects—reading, writing, and math—he was functioning at a third grade level.

Thus, when he left Sisters of Mercy on his nineteenth birthday, also required, he was barely literate. He couldn't read the newspaper or order from a menu, nor did he know how to manage money or use public transportation. Equally distressing, he had no friends, no family, and a minimum wage job washing dishes, ironically, at a fast food restaurant. With little to look forward to, he hated each day and sunk into a depression before turning to drugs to lift his mood. Heroin was his mood elevator of choice.

It wasn't long before Sonny was jobless and homeless, living under a highway with rats for roommates. He panhandled and earned a few dollars a day, and when he could, he sold dope to junkies in the neighborhood. This enabled him to buy a winter coat at a second hand store and a blanket for cold nights under the viaduct. For protection from local gangbangers, he bought a knife he used for target practice to see how many rats he could kill. Often, when he hadn't eaten for a few days, he survived by scrounging discarded food from trash bins behind restaurants and bakeries. By anyone's judgment, Sonny was a bum. An impoverished, black bum.

Sonny didn't know Mary McFale, but he had seen her walking her dog on the sidewalk adjacent to the viaduct. He stayed away, because he knew better than to talk to strangers, particularly white women, and he didn't like dogs. Then, Mary and her dog were murdered. Police found them in some bushes about ten yards off the street, near the viaduct. The dog had his throat slit, and Mary had been robbed, raped, and stabbed eight times with a jagged knife. Their blood mingled as they bled out on a patch of mud and stringy grass. Mary had a four month old fetus in her womb.

Soon, the police came for Sonny. They cuffed him, shoved him into the back of a squad car, and drove him to the county jail. They accused him of murdering Ms. McFale and her dog. "Ain't done the deed," Sonny said, but it didn't matter much, because he was just what was needed to close the case: a man without education or means, without an advocate or any type of support. And, he was black.

Black people make up 13% of our population. Since 1976, however, 43% of the people executed have been black, and the chances of execution increase when the victim is white. The words of a Texas police officer sum it up pretty well, despite the fact that he said them a generation ago. Confronted with two suspects in a murder case, one white and one black, he said, "One of you two is gonna hang for this. Since you're the nigger, you're elected." This astounding bigotry was directed at Clarence Brandley who was charged with the murder of a white high school girl. Brandley was later exonerated after ten years on death row.

Sonny's brief life was without joy or accomplishment. It was so empty that one wonders how many times he smiled before he died. For sure, he lived a meager existence at an orphanage and under a highway until his life was taken in one of the most inhumane ways possible. And we're still not even sure he committed the crime for which he was put to death.

Sonny Johnson never had a chance.

On Some Tuesdays in the Spring

Sonny Johnson lived under Highway 95
sharing space with feral cats and vermin
'til they moved his blanket to the county jail
because the Man said he murdered Mary McFale

he faced the court without a dollar in his pocket
next to a pale faced public defender who didn't give a damn
a jury found him guilty in less than three hours
and sentenced him to die on a Tuesday in the spring

fatty pork and greens cooled greasy on a tin plate
as a portly priest sanctified Sonny's soul
no stays of execution were offered up to save him
from being discarded like a mound of yesterday's trash

they bound him to the chair; "Old Sparky," they called it
and fastened electrodes to his limbs and head
beads of sweat on Sonny's forehead glistened
"ain't done the deed; how come y'all don't listen?"

the lights in the cell block flickered
and Sonny convulsed hard against his bindings
and smoke curled from his head
and his blood bubbled and boiled
and his eyeballs melted and popped from their sockets

and his organs fried to well done
and his bladder leaked hot urine
and they waited until his body cooled
before they put him in the ground

Sonny's fate is justified in some holy books
that tell us "an eye for an eye" is the way
but does anyone care how many men are taken
with the chilling chance we are mistaken
on some Tuesdays in the spring

That's Bullshit, Professor

I had a Master's Degree from the University of Illinois and two years teaching experience at a high school in an affluent suburb north of Chicago. The affluence was most evident by inspecting the cars in the student parking lot. They were much nicer than those in the faculty lot.

My students were mildly mentally retarded (the preferred term today is "developmentally delayed"), and I taught them very useful things like how to apply for a job, how to write a check, and how to shop at a supermarket. I also did what I could to encourage them to participate in the social and athletic activities offered by the school. I enjoyed the experience, but I wanted more. So in the spring, I checked out the requirements to get a Ph.D. in Special Education back at the University of Illinois.

The requirements were daunting, particularly for someone who had grown used to frequent visits to the quadrangle for games of frisbee or lazy naps in the sun. I would need to complete sixteen courses beyond the Master's, each requiring lengthy term papers or exercises in experimental design and statistical methods. On the side, I would need to demonstrate competency in French and German by translating articles in my field into English. Beyond that, I'd have to pass written qualifying examinations (based upon my coursework) taking eight hours a day for three consecutive days. Next, I'd have to develop a dissertation proposal and convince a five-member team of professors that my idea was valid. Should they favor me with their approval, I'd gather my data and write my dissertation—a process taking about two years. Finally, I would be required to defend my work in final orals before the same five-person committee and anyone from the general community who cared to drop in and hear me wax erudite. There was always the possibility, too, that I'd be asked to teach undergraduate courses at the same time as I was meeting all of my other requirements. Thus, one thing was certain. The University of Illinois was not about to grant me my doctorate because I was good looking.

Subsequently, I plunged in and got my degree in five years including summers, during which time there wasn't a whole lot of napping in the sun. There were, however, two babies to take care of. There are times when one needs a break from the books.

Armed with a Ph.D. and a young family but no job, I applied at a number of universities. One of them, Chicago State, had a new program in Special Education, and they had an opening for an assistant professor. They were looking for someone to teach courses about children and adolescents with developmental delays, learning disabilities, and emotional disorders as well as doing research in those areas.

It was not a prestigious university according to most standards; for example, the four-year graduation rate was low, and the number of students requiring remedial assistance in writing and math was high. It required a long commute, as well; however, I took the position when it was offered. "I'll give it a shot," I thought, "and if it doesn't work out, I'll look for something else."

It worked out for almost thirty-five years. In fact, it worked out so well that I never felt it was a job. Instead, it was fun, and I learned a tremendous amount from my students. Most of them were women who were teaching during the day at some of the most difficult schools in Chicago. The children in their classes came from poverty, and most of their homes were one-parent. The government sponsored free breakfast and lunch programs provided the only meals these children could count on. Many of them didn't have warm enough clothing, and some were obviously sleep deprived when they arrived in the morning. It's hard to teach children to read, write, and do math when their more basic needs aren't being met.

So, it's fair to say that my students had challenging jobs. Yet, after teaching from 8 a.m. to 3 p.m. every day, they enrolled in courses at the university. They did so in order to earn advanced degrees and a salary boost and to learn techniques they hoped would help them become more effective teachers. In any case, given that they had already worked full days, oftentimes under a good deal of stress, I felt it was my job to keep them interested from 5 to 7:50 during the evenings we met.

Three hours is a long time to sit in class, and if it's filled with nothing but professorial drone, what's going to happen is a lot of head bobbing and snoring among the audience. I vowed I wouldn't let that happen so, whenever possible, I inserted simulations and other demonstrations designed to keep my students enthused and involved, having a little fun whenever possible. I knew I was doing something right when a student approached me after class one evening and said, "You ought to sell tickets, Dr. B." It's an idea that had crossed my mind more than once, since there were many years when professors got a measly one or two percent raise in salary, and some years we got nothing. At the same time, the varsity basketball coach was always the highest paid faculty member on staff. It's a question of values.

About half my classes were held in large, traditional lecture halls. I stood at the bottom where the lectern and blackboard were, and my students sat in rows of seats that slanted upward. Typically, there would be anywhere from twenty-five to forty students enrolled, and very few had Y chromosomes.

Standing in front made me highly visible, so the last thing I did before entering the lecture hall was a fly check. There was a good chance, I felt, that "letting it all hang out," as it were, would appreciably distract my students from the material at hand. One evening, my pre-class inspection revealed that my zipper had broken and was irreparable.

Of course, I could have hidden behind the lectern for three hours, but I liked to move around in class. So, I decided upon a direct and frontal approach, so to speak. "Ladies," I said, "If you haven't already noticed, my fly is open. I can't fix it, so get your twittering out of the way, and let's move on."

From the third row, a large woman with a throaty chuckle said, "Don't worry Dr. B., it's no big deal."

"I'm not sure I'm happy with your choice of words," I said.

When I asked my students to tell me about the most difficult part of their day, they usually said it came down to classroom management. "I have good lesson plans, but a lot of times, I can't get through to my students because a few misbehave. What can I do?"

"You've got to catch them being good," I said. "All too often, the only behaviors we attend to are the bad ones, so those are the ones that kids repeat. Conversely, if you praise and reward them for behaving well and ignore the misbehavior, they're likely to repeat the good stuff."

From the rear, I heard a three-word proclamation, clearly enunciated and directly to my point. Her name was Felicia, and I've never forgotten her retort: "That's bullshit, Professor!"

When I asked for elucidation, I got a question in return: "When is the last time you taught in the Chicago Public Schools? If I ignore 'em, they'll walk all over me."

It was a quarter to 8, so I said we'd talk about it next time, and I ducked out of the lecture hall five minutes early. "Jeez," I thought; "Felicia has a point." Her point was so sharp, in fact, that it honed my professorial style forever.

Over the next few days, I conducted a survey in the College of Education at the university. Within five departments employing almost sixty professors, all of whom were involved to varying degrees in preparing teachers, I was astonished to discover that not a single professor had ever taught in the Chicago Public Schools. There we were, so called experts in urban education, physical education, educational administration, early childhood education, and special education, training teachers and principals, ninety percent of whom would go on and work in the Chicago Public Schools, and not a single one of us had ever been a teacher in those schools ourselves.

How could I have missed it? Teachers in training are taught by professors who never see children or, at best, haven't seen them since they fled their classrooms in affluent suburbs for the safety of the university. Indeed, at the university, there wasn't a child in sight, let alone a child of poverty.

The next day, I drove to the administrative offices of the Chicago Public Schools and applied for a job. My idea was to work in a grade school during the day and meet my responsibilities at the university during the evenings. I knew it would be exhausting, but I had no doubt it would make me a better professor.

Of course, I knew many of the people at the Board of Education. "What are you doing here?" one of them asked.

"I'm applying for a job," I said.

"Are you leaving the university?"

"No, I'll be there for office hours and my evening classes, but I want to work at a school during the day so I can see what's going on in the real world."

"Well, good luck Professor; you may be in for some surprises."

In class, a week later, I told my students what I was planning. They were enthused, particularly Felicia who had characterized my advice as "bovine fecal material" the week before. Indeed, the idea that one of their professors would be "going back to school" and gaining first-hand knowledge of what they were up against was unique, if not darn near heroic to their thinking.

At the time I applied for a job, I held State of Illinois certificates enabling me to teach children and adolescents who were developmentally delayed, learning disabled, or emotionally disturbed.

Apparently though, the city of Chicago, at least for the purpose of educating children with disabilities, didn't consider itself to be part of the State of Illinois, so they had their own certificates. Therefore, to work as a teacher of children with learning disabilities in a classroom in Chicago, I'd have to get a City of Chicago teaching certificate, and that meant I'd have to sit for the Chicago Board of Education examination.

There I was, a person who had taught graduate level courses in learning disabilities for years, who had consulted with more than a few school districts regarding learning disabilities, and who had published articles in the field, being asked to demonstrate that I knew some basic stuff. Initially, given my background and experience, I thought the Board of Education might consent to waive the requirement that I take their test. As I thought about it some more, however, I changed my mind. I didn't want any special treatment; rather, I wanted to go through the same steps as my students at the university were required to take. Thus, on a rainy Saturday morning, I sat for the examination. I opened it and chuckled to myself, because it was the same exam I had written for the Board of Education three years previously. I passed with no trouble at all, even missed a few on purpose so no one would accuse me of cheating.

It took about a month before all the paper work was completed, and I was assigned to an elementary school. A few of the teachers already working in the building had been students of mine at the university. So, when I showed up, they assumed I was a spy. They weren't entirely wrong. My plan was to work at the grade school for a year. In fact, it turned out to be seven years. Without question, the experience made me a more effective professor. Fact is, there was a ton of stuff going on that the old professor just didn't know was happening.

I observed a full range of teaching quality—some so good I would not hesitate to endorse it as masterful and some so bad it was embarrassing. The latter was exemplified by teachers passing out mindless worksheets and then retiring to their desks with a fresh cup of coffee and the morning newspaper; thus, chaos prevailed in their classrooms all day long. Many teachers in the bilingual program weren't bilingual, so their students never learned to speak English. Of course, these teachers should have been observed by the principal and given suggestions to improve their practice. Our principal, however, seldom made the rounds; in fact, during my seven-year tenure, three different principals never visited my classroom. Nor were any incompetent teachers fired.

Children with disabilities were segregated into one wing of the school as if their problems were contagious. That part of the school was known as "Horror Hall" and reminded me of the old days when people with disabilities were locked away in isolated institutions, away from the rest of the population. Without acceptable behaviors to imitate, the kids in Horror Hall only became more horrible.

Some had been labeled "ED," or emotionally disturbed, and others were called "BD," or behavior disordered. I couldn't tell the difference until one of my colleagues enlightened me. "The BD kids are the bad ones," she said, "and the ED kids are the crazy ones."

There were other incidents that were no less shocking. A fourteen-year-old girl in eighth grade had won the school oratory contest by delivering a very poignant reading of a poem about abortion. Because she won the school contest, she was eligible to participate at the regional level, that is, a contest at a neighboring school. To travel off campus, however, required parental permission. "I'll be glad to have my mother sign the permission slip," the girl said, "but you probably should know I have a daughter of my own at home. She was born last summer; here's a picture."

A seventh-grade boy who couldn't read served as a hall guard. I would see Calvin at his post almost every day and spend some time talking with him. "Calvin," I said, "would you like me to help you with your reading?"

"Nah, I don't care about that shit, but I can strip your car in about twenty minutes."

Calvin stopped coming to school after a while. I asked the principal about his whereabouts.

"Calvin is in jail," he said. "He and two of his buddies robbed, raped, and murdered a nurse. Chances are he'll never get out."

In fact, after five years, Calvin did get out when it was discovered that his confession had been coerced; that is, he confessed only after he was tortured by one of Chicago's more infamous men in blue. The officer went to jail, and Calvin was released with enough money to buy cars and drugs.

At school, I experienced the lack of professional respect granted to teachers when we were not trusted to keep custody of our students' records. Such records contained test results and educational plans that were supposed to help us become more effective, but they were kept locked up in the counselor's office. It's hard to imagine a physician needing to walk to a centrally located vault to check on the history of a patient.

The notion that teachers do not enjoy the same status as other professionals was further driven home when I learned that I had to punch in and out on a time clock every morning and afternoon. Only a hard hat and a lunch pail were missing.

In sum, I learned that in too many instances the education provided for children with disabilities was neither special nor was it education. At least as bad was the treatment of parents of children with disabilities. Often, they were given fallacious information, or their rights weren't explained. At meetings, where they were the most important people present, those who knew the most about their children, they were ignored and sat silently while the experts spouted their psychological jargon. "Your child has cognitive deficits in the verbal area compounded by visual and auditory perception problems along with attention deficits and transient hyperactivity." That's how they talk to parents, many of whom don't know English and never went to high school. It was shameful.

With respect to aging, it has been said that the days pass slowly, but the years pass quickly. So it seemed that, in a flash, I had become the senior faculty member in my department at the university, a person who had long since become a member of AARP, and someone who began thinking seriously about hanging up his chalk and erasers. The feeling was reinforced when one of my students informed me that her mother had been a student of mine a generation ago.

At my retirement dinner, I got a plaque and commendation from the Dean of the College of Education. During my last lecture, my "swan song," so to speak, I felt as if I had 'em in the palm of my hand. Also, there was no problem with my zipper.

On the thirty-seven-mile commute home that last time, I replayed as much as I could. It was a magnificent career because I had the opportunity to be with enthusiastic students who appreciated and benefitted from my efforts. Dozens of my students were teaching children with disabilities in public and private schools, and they were relying upon knowledge and techniques that I had taught them. I got to write, speak, and grow with gifted colleagues in an atmosphere where academic freedom prevailed.

One might say that the professor hung around in the corral for a while until finally learning to avoid the bullshit.

A Question of Values

When Bobby Falcone wasn't yet one, he began to speak
Along with English, he became fluent in French, Italian, and
Greek
Folks were stunned on his fourth birthday, those near
enough to hear him
Because Bobby Falcone was expounding upon a geometric
theorem

When other kids were riding their bikes and listening to CD's
Bobby was learning Biology with astonishing ease
And instead of taking his roller skates for a spin around the
block
He mastered pieces on the cello by Beethoven, Brahms, and
Bach

Going to regular school would have been a waste of time
Just about as wasteful as teaching Shakespeare to rhyme
So his parents employed some tutors to keep their son's
mind keen
And Bobby earned an MD from Yale the year he turned
nineteen

Promoted to full professor at Princeton University
The youngest in history because Bobby was only
twenty-three

Surgical techniques he invented and introduced to his field
Soon were implemented to help little brains get healed

Bobby practiced brain surgery at hospitals far and wide
While his family stood back and reveled with considerable
pride
And if ever some parents came to him who couldn't afford to
pay
It didn't matter to Bobby; he helped them anyway

Bobby is thirty now and directs a lab at a medical center
Working on curing brain cancer so little kids have a life to
enter
He ought to be a hero right there at the head of the pack
But hardly anyone cheers him, 'cause he doesn't play
quarterback

Penelope

If people come close to Penny, she feels vibrations. She hears a humming sound. She smells their scent and sees their aura. If they touch her, Penny hears their thoughts. They think Penny is pretty. They think Penny is strange. She makes people uncomfortable, because they have never known anyone like her. They're uneasy, anxious, even a little frightened. They're hoping she'll go away, because pretty Penny does peculiar things.

She stares at shiny objects. She spins them between her fingers. She licks cold metal. She plays with fire. She blows out candles and breathes the smoke. She never laughs or smiles or talks. Woolen clothes and rushing water hurt her skin. She doesn't like being touched. She smells music, and she can taste it too. She sees out of the sides of her eyes. She hears snowflakes and dust landing. Penny is so peculiar people have a name for her. They call her autistic.

Penny was a beautiful baby. She looked at her mother's eyes. She smiled and spoke to her mother. She loved her mother. Then, Penny stopped looking and smiling and speaking, and she broke her mother's heart. "It's not your fault, Mom. It was never your fault. Penny still loves you. She loves you more than ever."

Penny remembers being a young girl. She thinks everyone hears and sees the way she does. How is she to know what is normal when she has never experienced what is normal?

Now, Penny knows better. She knows her hearing, vision, and other senses are terribly acute. "Hypersensitive" is the word the doctors use. It's as if she hears, sees, smells, touches, and tastes too well. So, in Penny's world, there is no respite. It's like an assault.

A person tries to enter Penny's world with a question. At the same time, the clock is ticking. A faucet is dripping. Some children are playing outside, a truck is rumbling down the street, the wind is blowing some leaves, the kitchen windows are rattling, an ambulance is wailing, the refrigerator is humming, some clothes are tumbling in the dryer, the telephone is ringing, the toilet is running, and a dog is barking. Penny hears everything around her, but she doesn't respond to anyone's questions. Their voices are just one more sound competing for her attention, no more or less important than any of the other background noises. They're all persistent assailants in the same assault.

Most nights, Penny doesn't fall asleep easily. To her parents, the house is still. They don't hear the foundation settling, the nails loosening, or the floors sinking. They don't hear the bugs gnawing or the mice nibbling. They don't hear their eyelids blinking. They don't hear dust landing on their dressers and night stands.

It's not only the sounds from outside that keep her awake but sounds from inside her body as well. She hears her heart beating and blood coursing through her veins. She hears her intestines growling and her bile oozing. She hears her lungs expanding and deflating. Noises from swallowing bounce off her temples. In Penny's world, there is no escaping things. She gets no rest.

Penny sees sounds. They have flavors, they smell, she can feel them, and they move, too. Beethoven's Fifth Symphony is green. It feels cool and smooth, like satin on her skin. The music smells like wet grass, and it tastes like pears. It moves at a moderate pace, in rhythmic waves, from right to left. Dylan's Subterranean Homesick Blues is red. It feels hot and gritty on her skin. The music smells like garlic, and it tastes like barbecue. It moves in fits and starts from left to right with occasional spikes when it's loud.

Penny's eyesight is perfect, but her perception isn't. There is a large maple outside Penny's window, but she is unaware of the trunk, the branches, and the overall shape. She misses the essence of the tree, because she is riveted by the individual leaves. There is an ocean wave heading on shore. She doesn't perceive it as a swell of water, because she focuses on the individual droplets. There is a person standing next to her. She doesn't recognize your face, because she fixates on your pores. Penny is slow to perceive your whole because she can't get past your parts. A person shouldn't take it personally.

Penny's mother and father didn't know what to do. They took her to doctors, but they didn't know what to do either. Most of the doctors had never seen a child like Penny, because she's a member of a small minority group. Help fight segregation. Invite pretty Penny to dinner. A person should serve Penny soft food. Hard food makes too much noise when she chews, and it feels like stones in her mouth.

Penny and her parents went to a famous and learned professor who called himself a psychiatrist. He told Mother it was all her fault. She was aloof and mechanistic, more like a machine than a mother. She was cold, a "refrigerator woman," he called her. Subconsciously, she resented being pregnant, and she rejected pretty Penny from the moment she was born. Penny sensed her mother's rejection, and she withdrew into herself.

The famous and learned professor said all those things about Penny's mother. He said them with absolute conviction after he had known her for less than an hour. What a perceptive man he must have been. Or, maybe he wasn't.

The professor had an impeccable reputation. He was the foremost authority in his field. He professed at a prestigious university, and he wrote scholarly books. People are quick to assume that such an accomplished person must be right about everything. Penny's parents assumed he was right. Other parents of autistic children assumed he was right. Everyone but Penny assumed he was right. His aura was very thin, almost invisible.

Penny's mother took the blame. Then, the famous professor convinced her parents that Penny wouldn't get better unless she left her home and family. The professor wanted her to live at his special school. His school was in a big city, far from Penny's home. Penny would have to be separated from the people she loved. The professor had a curious word for busting up families. He called it a "parentectomy."

Penny knew her mother and father were desperate. They were ready to try anything that might help her. They wondered what kind of parents they would be if they didn't do what the professor advised. So, they helped her pack her belongings. They took her to the professor's far away school and said goodbye. After all, such a perceptive man must be worthy of trust. Or, maybe he wasn't.

It was two months before Mother stopped weeping during the day. She never stopped at night. Father put up a brave front, but inside he was melancholy. Their child was gone; he missed her, and he felt a terrible sadness. Penny was hundreds of miles away; still, she knew how her parents suffered.

There were no classrooms, no desks, and no blackboards at the professor's special school. Some days the teachers didn't prepare any lessons, and the students didn't follow any rules. The air felt thick and brown, polluted, and it smelled like rubbing alcohol, but Penny remained at the school while the professor and his loyal band of assistants practiced their "psychiatric stuff" to make her less peculiar. When that didn't work out so well, they practiced child abuse.

Penny lived at the professor's school for two years. She lived with other autistic children who came from across the country. Their parents were desperate and eager to try anything, too.

When Penny and her mates weren't being practiced upon, they had plenty of time to wonder what their refrigerators were doing. For two years, Penny never saw her parents. Not once. Even written correspondence was forbidden. The professor excised Mom and Dad from her life, just as he said he would.

Penny got no better, so Mom and Dad started questioning the professor. They didn't like his answers. They stopped trusting him, and they decided to bring Penny home. With all his insight, the professor wanted Penny to stay at his place for two more years. "These things take some time," he said.

Mom wasn't willing to give him any more time. "You've had our child long enough," she said.

Foremost authorities get to be adamant, so the professor was persistent. He looked surprised when Dad narrowed his eyes and quietly told him to go to hell. Dad wanted to hurt him. Penny saw and smelled her father's rage. It was red-orange, and it reeked of burning rubber. The professor stopped being so adamant.

A few years later, the famous and learned professor from the prestigious university got depressed. No one knows for sure why he killed himself. Perhaps other people got suspicious. Maybe other people stopped trusting him. Maybe he felt guilty because he had not always been kind to children. Maybe he could no longer stand knowing the truth—that under his skin there was a mean and bigoted man, a man who wasn't a psychiatrist at all, a man who was an impostor, a fraud, a man who built his impeccable reputation on a foundation of lies. Whatever the reason, the professor did himself in; he kicked the oxygen habit, a person might say. Or a person might say he performed a "selfectomy."

The professor was wrong about everything. Penny's mother was a brave, sweet woman who loved her as much as any woman ever loved her child. She loved Penny from the first, fiercely, without reservation, never stopping, not for a second. Every day and every night of her life, she got down on her knees and prayed for Penny to get better. Refrigerator mother indeed. A person cannot break a refrigerator's heart.

Now, at last, the doctors know better. They know it's not mechanical mothering or any other psychological factor that makes Penny the way she is. Some doctors think certain chemicals may be out of balance in Penny's brain. Others think parts of Penny's brain may be damaged or that Penny's problems are genetic. And, research is beginning to indicate that some children with autism may have abnormal chromosomes, just like children with Down Syndrome.

It will probably be a while before the doctors discover the exact cause. Perhaps they will discover more than one cause. But, until the doctors finish their good work, at least a person can stop blaming Penny's mother. Penny's mother never did anything wrong. It's not your fault, Mom. It was never your fault. Penny still loves you. She loves you more than ever.

A Safer Place

on a planet a million light years away
where the air is warm and pure
four moons, each pastel in color,
spread soft night light across the land

two golden suns and sweet tasting rain
nourish flora in abundance
so a riot of color adorns each day
like a tapestry in a house of royals

otters swim in fresh water seas
and frolic with baby seals unafraid
and white tailed fawns feast on succulent plants
in purple forests all dewy and lush

the people differ in color too
maroon skinned, orange, and blue
their children play on fields of thick grass
some speaking while others are mute

they go to school happy each day
to learn what is false and true
never feeling the terrible threat of abuse
for licking a piece of cold steel

so wander with me on this world afar
where the others will come to love us
where no matter how different we happen to be
no one will blame our mothers

Richard

Sixty years ago, Richard would have been called "feebleminded." Before that, he would have been an "imbecile." Now, the preferred terms are "developmentally delayed" or "cognitively challenged." Euphemisms come and go with each generation, but no matter the terminology, Richard will be slow to learn for as long as he lives.

On the first day of Richard's life, his parents were told he was a mongoloid. The nurses put him in an isolated section of the hospital nursery, away from the viewing windows, so nobody could see him. Until she insisted, his mother was not allowed to feed him. The doctor advised placement in an institution. "These things are always difficult," he said, "but the separation will be easier if you do it immediately, before any bonding occurs." Then, the doctor went home to play with his children.

Richard's parents did some research. They learned there were still some people who were mentally retarded living in large institutions located in isolated rural areas. There, away from public scrutiny, they were crammed into wards with 100 roommates, give or take a few. This unnatural way of living made it easy for them to imitate each other's deviant behaviors. Thus, they grew ever more deviant. Together, they became institutionalized.

It was acceptable for them to be deprived of any form of recreational or training program. They were kept indoors, stagnating on their backs, bedsores festering, all the while staring at blank ceilings until the next attendant came to change their diapers. Sometimes, the next attendant, often a person working for minimum wage and unemployable elsewhere, was late or neglected to come to work at all, so the "retardates," as they were called, played with their feces and smeared it on the walls. Or, they ate it.

It was acceptable for them to be stripped naked and strapped upright to the walls of a special bathing room with seven or eight of their mates. The room was flooded, shoulder high, for their weekly bath. After a few minutes, the dirty water was flushed, and attendants dried them and dressed them in their next outfits. Whether their clothes were the right size or even gender appropriate didn't matter much. They simply wore whatever items of clothing were on the top of the pile.

It was acceptable to sterilize them without consent, too. "Eugenics," it was called, a method for improving the human race by the calculated selection of parents. The idea was to make it impossible for mentally retarded people to have children, thus effectively eliminating their kind in the relatively brief span of a few decades. Sieg Heil!

Depriving people who were mentally retarded of any semblance of dignity was justified by assuming they were so lacking in awareness as to be oblivious to their surroundings and treatment. What the heck. If they don't know what's going on, what difference does it make? One must wonder how it can be that a house pet, say a cocker spaniel, is aware of its surroundings and treatment, but a person, even a person who is mentally retarded, isn't?

"Surplus population" is a term that was appropriate. In the bad old days, the mentally retarded were treated as if they were a freakish overstock, a mutated species somewhere between the great apes and modern man on the phylogenetic scale, to be discarded, mistreated or, at best, ignored.

Richard's parents took their concerns about institutionalization to the doctor. "Oh, it's not like that anymore," he said. "Many of the old institutions, 'human warehouses,' as they were, have been closed, and smaller, community based facilities have taken their place. As a way of replacing institutionalization with a more natural, family style living arrangement, only small groups of people, usually no more than twelve, live under the same roof. They live in rooms, not wards, and parent surrogates assist in providing for their needs."

"Thank you all the same," Richard's parents replied. "We'll be taking our baby home with us."

Fast forward nineteen years, and meet Richard:

Some people call me Dicky, but my real name is Richard. I'm a grown up guy now, zackly nineteen and a half years old, so I don't like it too much when people call me Dicky. My real name is Richard. Ever one should call me Richard.

A little while back, prolly a month ago on that paper that has the days and weeks on it, I moved to this new place to live. A group home is what you call it. So far, I like livin' here pretty good. There's a lotta other people, a group of zackly thirteen or fourteen if you count ever single person besides me. Ever now and then, mostly when I'm alone tryin' to fall asleep at night, I miss my mom and dad and the house where I used to live all those years before I was a grown up guy, but

I'm doin' pretty good at my new house, the group home I'm talkin' bout. Yessir. Pretty darn good, I'd say.

When I was still livin' at the house where I grew up, I had a friend Billy that lived acrost the street. He tole me that it was a good idea for ever person to have at lease three wishes bout his hopes and dreams. Not two wishes or four wishes but zackly three. So, I think grown up guys, even old geezers with wrinkles, should still have hopes and dreams. That's what I think all right. So here I go with my first wish. You can never tell when a wish will come true. Yessir, you can never tell.

My first wish is that I didn't look like me. I know I can't do too much bout how I look, but that don't mean I have to like it. I don't even like to see myself in a mirror lest I really have to, like when I shave off my whickers or comb my hairs in the mornin'. And, even then, I try to finish up as fast as I can.

My eyes are kind of slanted, so when I laugh or smile, they look like slits. My nose is flattened out and takes up way too much room on my face. And, my mouth don't look so good neither. My tongue is too big, and there are some cracks on the top of it. Lots of times, special when I'm not thinkin' bout it, it will hang out of my mouth. Usual it hangs to the left or to the right, but never out the middle. I don't know why that is, so I asked dad, but he didn't know neither.

My hairs started fallin' out when I was still in high school, and now, cept for a few long ones that I comb over the top of my head and some fuzz round the sides and back, it's almost all gone. Most times, lease when I'm outside, I wear one of them sailor hats so people won't be able to tell I don't have too much hair on top. Sometimes, I wonder where all that hair goes when it falls off my head. Prolly down the drain or blown off by the wind when I'm not lookin'.

Gettin' back to how I look, it's not that I'm pure ugly or nothin' like that. I mean, people don't scream or run away like I'm a monster man or freak of some kind that you usual see next to the lady with the beard or the dog with two heads at the circus. But, I know I'm not one of those handsome guys neither. Let's just say I'm sure as can be that nobody is never goin' to ask me to be a movie star, cept maybe Dr. Cory that calls me a "slick lookin' dude" ever time he sees me. Case I didn't say so yet, Dr. Cory looks after me ever time I need some help with one of my prollems that mom or dad can't fix. Dad says he likes him, Dr. Cory I'm talkin' about, 'cause he's the kind of doctor that really cares about kids and don't charge an arm and a leg or any other part of you, I guess.

Well, now that you know what I look like, which ain't too great, it's time for my second wish. There's no reason my second wish can't come true, even if it ain't the first one on my list. Yessir, you can never tell about wishes; that's what I think.

Anyways, my second wish is that I could learn how to read. When I was a kid, I tried to learn to read over and over, almost without a break, but even with special tutors, usual old ladies with glasses and perfume that smelled up my house after school and sometimes on Saturday too, I never got that good at it. Seems like what I learned from the tutor one time, I forgot by the next time she came around. So there I was, still pretty crummy at readin', with an old lady in my house that prolly wanted to be somewheres else with a kid that could read better.

After tryin' to learn to read so many times, a lot of guys would just throw in the towel. Dad says that thing about the towel, the throwin' in part, even though I never have one to throw in when I'm gettin' my latest readin' lesson. I could prolly get one, a towel I'm talkin' bout, but I wouldn't throw it in anyways. That's the kind of guy I am.

Sometimes, I see little kids that are even younger than me already readin' and writin' like it's a snap for them. I mean, they just go along readin' and writin' as easy as breathin' in and out.

When I see them little kids doin' what I can't do so good yet, I usual get down on myself for a while. I'd say I feel somewhere between sad and mad, prolly closer to sad.

Well, I bet you're wonderin' bout my third wish. I'm the kind of guy that doesn't like to tell what he knows all at the same time. I been tryin' to keep you guessin' is what I'm sayin', and if you keep payin' attention, I'll be ready to tell you my bout my last wish, the third one.

When I was in grade school and high school, I went to a special class. It was for kids that didn't learn so fast and needed a small class of zackly eight or ten kids, so the teacher could give each of us more time. What a bunch we had. Five of the kids looked just like me with the slanted eyes, big noses, and tongues that hung out from their mouths, usual to the left or right. You prolly know by this time that we all looked the same 'cause we all had Down Syndrome. Yessir. We coulda been twins or at lease brothers and sisters in the same family, that's how much we looked like each other.

Another guy, Victor was his name, had this very big head and couldn't see very good neither. I mean, his head was a doozy all right, so big and heavy that he could hardly hold it up straight. He couldn't talk neither, cept for some grunting sounds that he did when he was smearing spit on the top of his desk. The amazin' thing about Victor, though, was that he could play ever tune you could possible think of on the piano. I mean, alls he had to do was hear it one time, a tune I'm talkin' bout, and he could play it perfeck from then on. Not even the teachers, all them smart ladies that went to college, could figure it out.

Audrey was a girl who had a long scar on her head, almost from one ear to the other. Teacher tole us it was 'cause she had bout half her brains cut out 'cause of some kind of bad thing growin' up in there. Her legs didn't work so good, so she had to sit in a wheelchair all day. And her arms weren't so strong neither, so she moved around by breathin' into a tube that made her wheels move forward, back, or any which away. I always wanted to give Audrey's chair a try, but she didn't like to share too much. I didn't blame her, cause nobody wants someone else's spit in their tube.

I think the strangest of all my classmates was Penelope. She was the most prettiest girl I ever saw with straight yellow hair hangin' to the middle of her back, blue eyes the color of the sky when it ain't rainin', and a perfeck small nose that was just right for the size of her face. She had the kind of skin that looked very smooth to me and didn't have any pimples on it or even any rough spots. When somthin' is that smooth, you could say it's like silk.

But, thing is, Penny never talked to me. Even if I went right up close to her and asked her, in my best manners and with a nice soft voice how she was feelin', or if things were cool, or if I could carry her books, she just didn't answer me.

After a while, I got to thinkin' Penny didn't have a tongue, til one day on the school bus. I took a quick peek at her, and I saw her stick out her tongue and lick the metal handle on the seat in front of her. She hardly never looked at me neither, cept sometimes out of the corners of her eyes.

In my dreams, I take some money out of the bank and ask Penny to come with me for a date. We go to a movie about some guys shootin' rays at the people on Earth that turns 'em into rocks, and after the movie, we go to a restaurant for a large pizza and some Cokes or lemonade, either one. I have some funny jokes and stories ready to tell her in perfeck speech, and on the walk home, we hold each other's hands. When we get to her front door, we have some hugs like good friends usual do.

After our hugs like good friends usual do, Penny finally smiles and says thank you, out loud I'm sayin', for the good time she had. Then, she gives me her phone number so I can call her up if I ever feel lonely or just want to have a talk.

That was my dream all right, and that was my third wish. It will prolly never come true, but I won't give up. That's the kind of guy I am.

Waiting

men were pacing, anxious and eager
to pass out cigars when their babies came
then, alone on a well-worn, wicker chair
I waited for ours

she would be pretty with yellow hair
graceful as a ballerina poised on her toes
or he would be tall and fleet afoot
standing across the yard pitching a curve ball

a gray haired nurse ran her hand through my hair
then hugged me with arms soft and smooth
gentle in her manner, her name was Rachel
"I'm so very sorry," she said, "your baby isn't well"

"leave him with strangers far away
before he gets to know you," the doctor said
then I looked into my son's eyes, and it seemed to me
he already did

so, don't worry little boy; you're coming home with us
to the crib I built for you and a kid sized rocking horse
and soon we'll be rolling in the soft snow out back
but first, I have these cigars

About the Author

Alan Balter was born in Chicago and attended the Chicago Public Schools. He matriculated at the University of Illinois in Urbana in 1956 and earned a Bachelor's Degree in Psychology (1960) and a Master's Degree in Special Education (1962). He taught adolescents with developmental delays at Niles Township High School West for two years before returning to the University of Illinois and completing a Ph.D. in Special Education in 1967. While completing his degree, he taught undergraduate courses at the University. He went on to enjoy a 32 year tenure at Chicago State University where he prepared teachers for children with special needs.

Dr. Balter has published two nonfiction books: *Divided Apple: A Story about Teaching in Chicago* and *Learning Disabilities: A Book for Parents*, both with Kendall-Hunt publishers. He has also published two novels: *Holden and Me* (Rockway Press), for which he received their international fiction award in 2006 and *Different Ways of Being* (Linkville Press, 2013). His essay, "Cruel and Unusual Endings," about physician assisted suicide, appeared in the Op-Ed section of the *Chicago Tribune* in 2000. Additionally, he has published *Poetry for My Grandchildren and Everyone Else's* (Infinity Press, 2011) and *Melancholia, a Poetry Chapbook.* (Kelsay Books, 2020).

Dr. Balter and his wife Barbara, also a retired teacher, live in Northbrook, Illinois. They enjoy extensive travel and 14 grandchildren.

Apprentice
House Press
Loyola University Maryland

Apprentice House is the country's only campus-based, student-staffed book publishing company. Directed by professors and industry professionals, it is a nonprofit activity of the Communication Department at Loyola University Maryland.

Using state-of-the-art technology and an experiential learning model of education, Apprentice House publishes books in untraditional ways. This dual responsibility as publishers and educators creates an unprecedented collaborative environment among faculty and students, while teaching tomorrow's editors, designers, and marketers.

Outside of class, progress on book projects is carried forth by the AH Book Publishing Club, a co-curricular campus organization supported by Loyola University Maryland's Office of Student Activities.

Eclectic and provocative, Apprentice House titles intend to entertain as well as spark dialogue on a variety of topics. Financial contributions to sustain the press's work are welcomed. Contributions are tax deductible to the fullest extent allowed by the IRS.

To learn more about Apprentice House books or to obtain submission guidelines, please visit www.apprenticehouse.com.

Apprentice House Press
Communication Department
Loyola University Maryland
4501 N. Charles Street
Baltimore, MD 21210
Ph: 410-617-5265
info@apprenticehouse.com
www.apprenticehouse.com